SCHOLAST

File-Folder Games *in COLOR*
Alphabet

by Susan Julio

New York • Toronto • London • Auckland • Sydney
Mexico City • New Delhi • Hong Kong • Buenos Aires

Teaching *Resources*

Cover design by Jason Robinson
Interior design by Solas
Cover and interior illustrations by Rusty Fletcher

ISBN-13: 978-0-439-46591-5
ISBN-10: 0-439-46591-5

Contents

About This Book 4

Making & Using the File-Folder Games. 5

What the Research Says 6

Meeting the Language Arts Standards 6

File-Folder Games

Ship-Shape Letters (*letter shapes*). 7

Capital Letter Quilt (*matching uppercase letters*) 21

ABC Hives (*matching uppercase and lowercase letters*) 35

Busy Alphabet Beavers (*identifying uppercase and lowercase letters*) 49

Sky Writers (*writing uppercase and lowercase letters*) 61

Line Up for Recess! (*alphabetical order*). 75

Consonants in the Castle (*initial consonants*) 89

Give a Pup a Bone (*final consonants*). 105

Short Vowel Picnic Ants (*short vowels*) 119

Long Vowel Owl (*long vowels*). 131

About This Book

File-Folder Games in Color: Alphabet offers an engaging and fun way to motivate children of all learning styles and help build their letter knowledge and phonemic awareness. Research shows that understanding the alphabetic principle (that the letters of our alphabet stand for a series of sounds) is a critical first step in learning to read. In addition, the games in this book will help children meet important language arts standards. (See What the Research Says and Meeting the Language Arts standards, page 6, for more.)

The games are a snap to set up and store: Just tear out the full-color game boards from this book, glue them inside file folders, and you've got ten instant learning center activities. Children will have fun as they match uppercase and lowercase letters in ABC Hives, write letters of the alphabet in Sky Writers, match letters to their initial consonant sounds in Consonants in the Castle, identify short vowels in Short Vowel Picnic Ants, and much more.

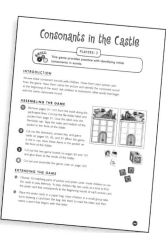

What's Inside

Each game includes the following:

- an introductory page for the teacher that provides a suggestion for introducing the game

- step-by-step assembly directions

- Extending the Game activities to continue reinforcing children's skills and interest

- a label with the title of each game for the file-folder tab

- a pocket to attach to the front of the file folder for storing the game parts

- directions that explain to children how to play the game

- an answer key

- game cards

- one or more game boards

- some games also include game markers and a game cube or spinner

Making the File-Folder Games

In addition to the game pages, you will need the following:

- 10 file folders (in a variety of colors, if possible)
- scissors
- clear packing tape
- glue stick or rubber cement
- paper clips
- brass fasteners

Tips

- Back the spinners, game cubes, and game markers with tagboard before assembling. Laminate for durability.
- Before cutting apart the game cards, make additional copies (in color or black and white) for use with the Extending the Game activities.
- Place the accessories for each game, such as spinners, game cubes, and game markers in separate, labeled zipper storage bags. Keep the bags in a basket near the games.

Using the File-Folder Games

- Before introducing the games to children, conduct mini-lessons to review the letters and concepts used in each game.
- Model how to play each game. You might also play it with children the first time.
- Give children suggestions on how to determine the order in which players take turns, such as rolling a die and taking turns in numerical order.
- Store the games in a literacy center and encourage children to play in pairs or small groups before or after school, during free-choice time, or when they have finished other tasks.
- Send the games home for children to play with family members and friends.
- Use the Extending the Game activities to continue reinforcing children's skills and interest.

Storage Ideas

Keep the file-folder games in any of these places:

- learning center
- vertical file tray
- file box
- file cabinet
- bookshelf
- plastic stacking crate

What the Research Says

In his book *Phonics From A to Z*, reading specialist Wiley Blevins notes that the two best predictors of early reading success are alphabet recognition and phonemic awareness (Adams, 1990; Stanovich, 1992; Chall, 1996; Beck and Juel, 1995; Share, Jorm, Maclean, and Matthews, 1984). These two skills—knowing the letters and the sounds they represent and being able to identify these sounds with automaticity—are essential for early reading development.

Source: *Phonics From A to Z* by Wiley Blevins (Scholastic, 2006, revised)

Meeting the Language Arts Standards

Connections to the McREL Language Arts Standards

Mid-continent Research for Education and Learning (McREL), a nationally recognized nonprofit organization, has compiled and evaluated national and state standards—and proposed what teachers should provide for their PreK–K students to grow proficient in language arts. This book's games and activities support the following standards:

Uses the general skills and strategies of the reading process including:

- Knows uppercase and lowercase letters of the alphabet

- Uses basic elements of phonetic analysis (e.g., understands sound-symbol relationships; beginning and ending consonants, vowel sounds) to decode unknown words

Uses grammatical and mechanical conventions in written compositions including:

- Uses conventions of print in writing (e.g., forms letters in print, uses uppercase and lowercase letters of the alphabet)

Source: Kendall, J. S. & Marzano, R. J. (2004). *Content knowledge: A compendium of standards and benchmarks for K–12 education.* Aurora, CO: Mid-continent Research for Education and Learning Online database: http://www.mcrel.org/standards-benchmarks/

Connections to Early Childhood Language Arts Standards

The activities in this book are also designed to support you in meeting the following PreK–K literacy goals and recommendations established in a joint position statement by the National Association for the Education of Young Children (NAEYC) and the International Reading Association (IRA):

- Understands that print carries a message

- Engages in reading and writing attempts

- Recognizes letters and letter-sound matches

- Begins to write

Source: *Learning to Read and Write: Developmentally Appropriate Practices for Young Children,* a joint position statement of the International Reading Association (IRA) and the National Association for the Education of Young Children (NAEYC). http://www.naeyc.org/about/positions/pdf/PSREAD98.PDF © 1998 by the National Association for the Education of Young Children

Ship-Shape Letters

PLAYERS: 2

 SKILL

This game provides practice in identifying uppercase letters and their shapes.

INTRODUCTION

Write several uppercase letters on the chalkboard. Invite volunteers to name the letters and then trace around their shapes. Help children describe and compare the configurations. Repeat with other sets of letters. Finally, explain that knowing the shape of a letter can help children identify and even write letters.

ASSEMBLING THE GAME

1 Remove pages 9–19 from the book along the perforated lines. Cut out the file-folder label and pocket from page 9. Glue the label onto the file-folder tab. Tape the sides and bottom of the pocket to the front of the folder.

2 Cut out the directions, answer key, and game cards on pages 11 and 13. When the game is not in use, store these items in the pocket on the front of the folder.

3 Cut out the two game boards on pages 15 and 17 and glue them to the inside of the folder.

4 Cut out and assemble the game spinner on page 19.

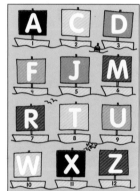

EXTENDING THE GAME

◎ Use a number die in place of the spinner. Tell players they can make matches on either game board. Then have them take a dried bean (or other counter) for each correct match they make. The game ends when all the sails are covered with cards. The player with the most counters wins.

◎ Frame a word or group of letters that occurs in print around the room. Have children find and name any uppercase letters in the framed text. Then call out any letter in the framed text. Have children search the room to see how many times they can find that letter in uppercase print.

Ship-Shape Letters

GET READY TO PLAY

- Each player chooses a game board.
- Shuffle the cards. Place them facedown.

TO PLAY

1 Spin the spinner. Take that number of cards.

2 Name the letter on each card. Do you see the shape of that letter on one of your sailboats?

- If so, put the card on the sail.
- If not, put the card on the bottom of the stack.

3 After each turn, check the answer key. Is each answer correct? If not, put that card on the bottom of the stack.

4 Keep taking turns. The first player to cover all of his or her sails wins the game.

Ship-Shape Letters

ANSWER KEY

Game Board 1 (left side)

1. B	**2.** E	**3.** G
4. I	**5.** K	**6.** L
7. N	**8.** P	**9.** Q
10. S	**11.** V	**12.** Y

Game Board 2 (right side)

1. A	**2.** C	**3.** D
4. F	**5.** J	**6.** M
7. R	**8.** T	**9.** U
10. W	**11.** X	**12.** Z

A	B	C	D
E	F	G	I
J	K	L	M
N	P	Q	R
S	T	U	V
W	X	Y	Z

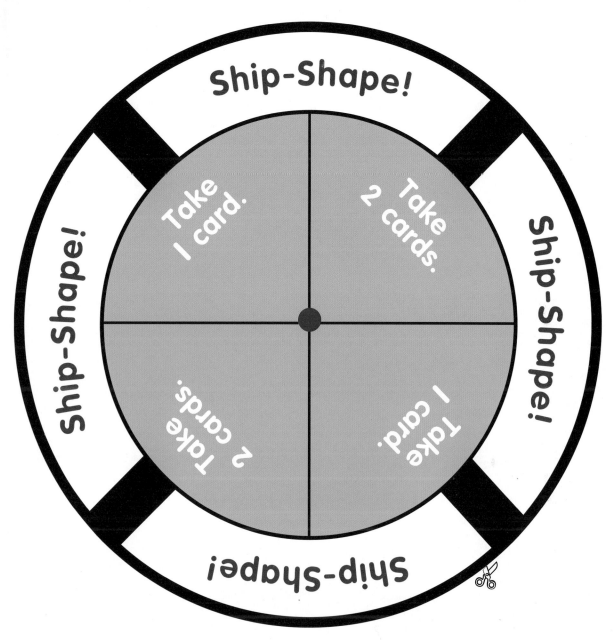

Ship-Shape!

Ship-Shape!

Ship-Shape!

Ship-Shape!

Take 1 card.

Take 2 cards.

Take 1 card.

Take 2 cards.

brass fastener

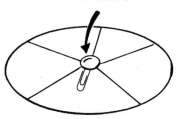

Assemble the spinner using a paper clip and brass fastener as shown. Make sure the paper clip spins easily.

Ship-Shape Letters Game Spinner 19

Capital Letter Quilt

PLAYERS: 2

This game provides practice in identifying uppercase letters of the alphabet.

INTRODUCTION

Using a set of alphabet cards, show children one uppercase letter at a time. Show the letters in alphabetical sequence. (Or point to each uppercase letter on an alphabet chart.) Ask children to name each letter. Afterward, show them uppercase letters in random order to identify.

ASSEMBLING THE GAME

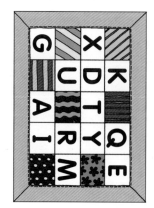
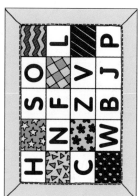

1 Remove pages 23–33 from the book along the perforated lines. Cut out the file-folder label and pocket from page 23. Glue the label onto the file-folder tab. Tape the sides and bottom of the pocket to the front of the folder.

2 Cut out the directions, answer key, and game cards on pages 25 and 27. When the game is not in use, store these items in the pocket on the front of the folder.

3 Cut out the two game boards on pages 29 and 31 and glue them to the inside of the folder.

4 Cut out and assemble the game spinner on page 33.

EXTENDING THE GAME

◎ Show children one uppercase letter card at a time. Have them identify the letter. Then ask children to search print in the room to find words that begin with the letter.

◎ Trim 26 index cards to the same size as the game cards. Write a different uppercase letter on each card. Place all the cards faceup on a table near the game board. On a signal, have two players try to be the first one to find and place all the matching letter cards on his or her game board.

Capital Letter Quilt

GET READY TO PLAY

Each player chooses a game board and 13 quilt-square cards.

TO PLAY

1 Spin the spinner. Name the two letters it lands on.
Is one of the letters on your quilt?

- If so, cover the letter with a card.
- If not, your turn ends.

2 After each turn, check the answer key. Is your answer correct?
If not, take the card back.

3 Keep taking turns. The first player to cover all of his or her letters
wins the game.

PLAYING TIP

Players may place only one quilt square on each letter.

Capital Letter Quilt

ANSWER KEY

Game Board 1 (left side)	Game Board 2 (right side)
K, Q, E	H, S, O
X, D, T, Y	N, F, L
U, R, M	C, Z, V
G, A, I	W, B, J, P

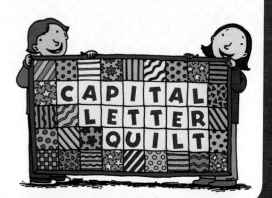

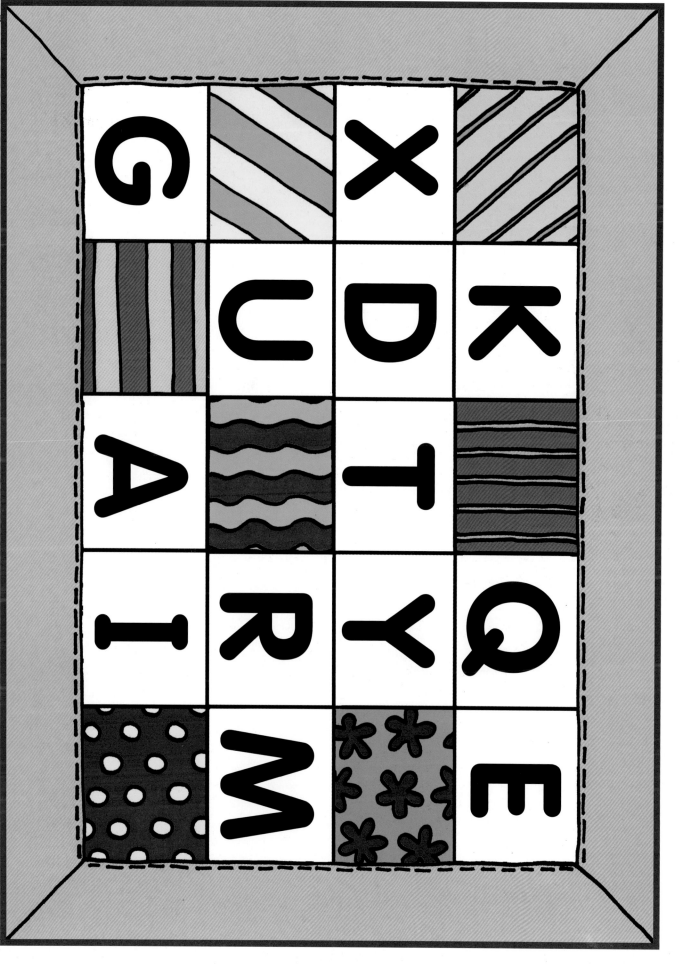

Glue this page to the left side of the file folder.

Capital Letter Quilt Game Board 1, page 29

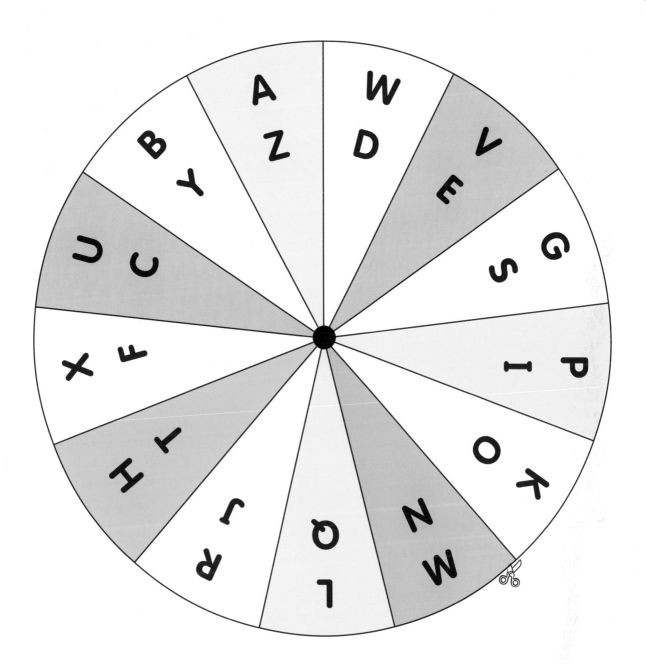

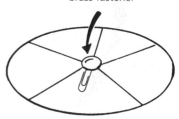

brass fastener

Assemble the spinner using a paper clip and brass fastener as shown. Make sure the paper clip spins easily.

ABC Hives

SKILL This game provides practice in matching uppercase and lowercase letters.

INTRODUCTION

Make a set of cards for the lowercase letters only. Cover the lowercase letters on an alphabet chart (trimmed sticky notes work well). Then show children one letter card at a time. Have them identify the letter and find the matching uppercase on the chart. Finally, uncover the lowercase letter to let children check their answer.

ASSEMBLING THE GAME

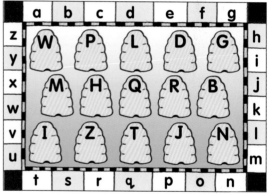

1. Remove pages 37–47 from the book along the perforated lines. Cut out the file-folder label and pocket from page 37. Glue the label onto the file-folder tab. Tape the sides and bottom of the pocket to the front of the folder.

2. Cut out the directions, answer key, and game cards on pages 39 and 41. Place each set of cards in a separate zipper storage bag. When the game is not in use, store these items in the pocket on the front of the folder.

3. Cut out the two sides of the game board on pages 43 and 45 and glue them to the inside of the folder.

4. Cut out and assemble the game cube and game markers on page 47.

EXTENDING THE GAME

◎ Make a separate set of cards for the uppercase and lowercase letters. Put the lowercase letter cards in a paper bag. Then spread the uppercase letter cards faceup on a table. Invite children to draw cards from the bag, name the lowercase letter, and find the matching uppercase letter.

◎ Write the uppercase and lowercase letters for 10–12 letter pairs on plain index cards. Invite children to use the cards to play Memory. To play, children flip two cards at a time to find the matching uppercase and lowercase letters.

ABC Hives

GET READY TO PLAY

- Each player chooses a game marker and a set of bee cards.
- Place each marker on any red corner on the game board.

TO PLAY

1 Roll the game cube. Move that number of spaces.

2 If the space has a letter, name it. Do you see the matching uppercase letter on a bee hive?
  - If so, place a bee on the hive.
  - If not, put the card on the bottom of the stack.

3 After each turn, check the answer key. Is your answer correct? If not, take the bee back.

4 Keep taking turns. Play continues until all of the hives are covered. The player with the most bees on the hives wins the game.

PLAYING TIPS

- Players may land on and share the same space.
- Players may move around the game board as many times as necessary.

ABC Hives

ANSWER KEY

B b	N n
D d	P p
G g	Q q
H h	R r
I i	T t
J j	W w
L l	Z z
M m	

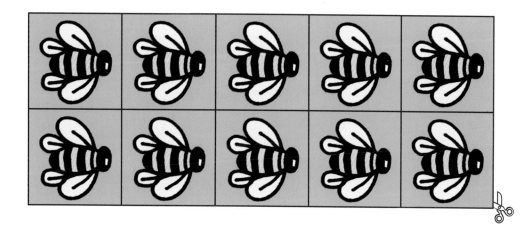

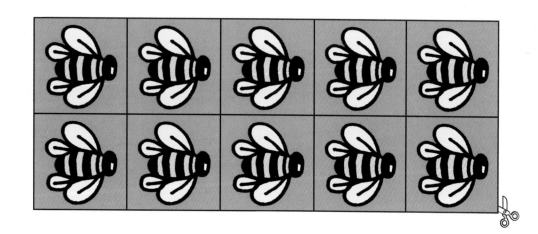

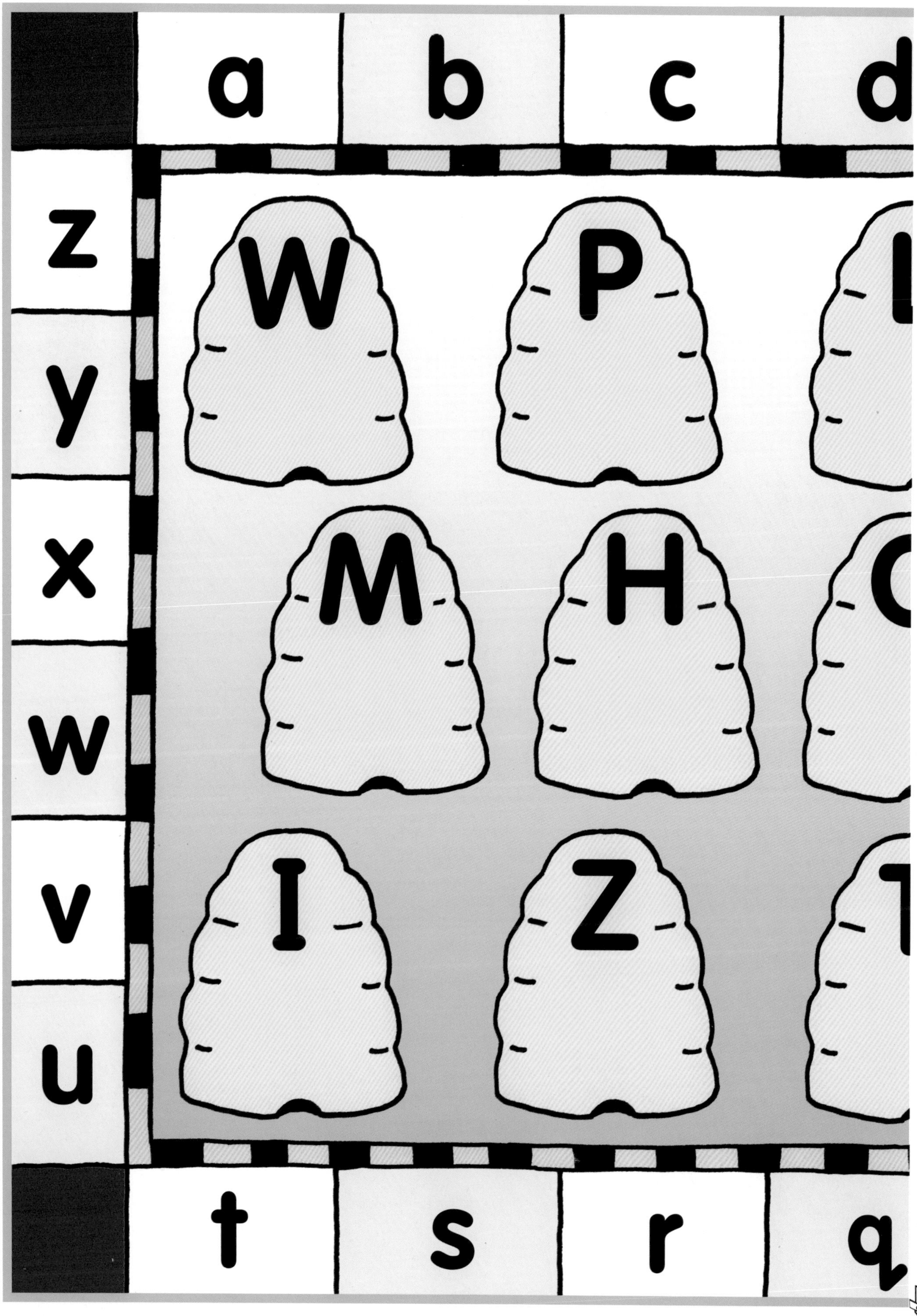

| a | b | c | d |

z

y

x

w

v

u

W

P

P

M

H

C

I

Z

T

t s r q

Cut along this edge and attach to page 45.

e f g

h

i

j

k

l

m

D G

Q R B

J N

p o n

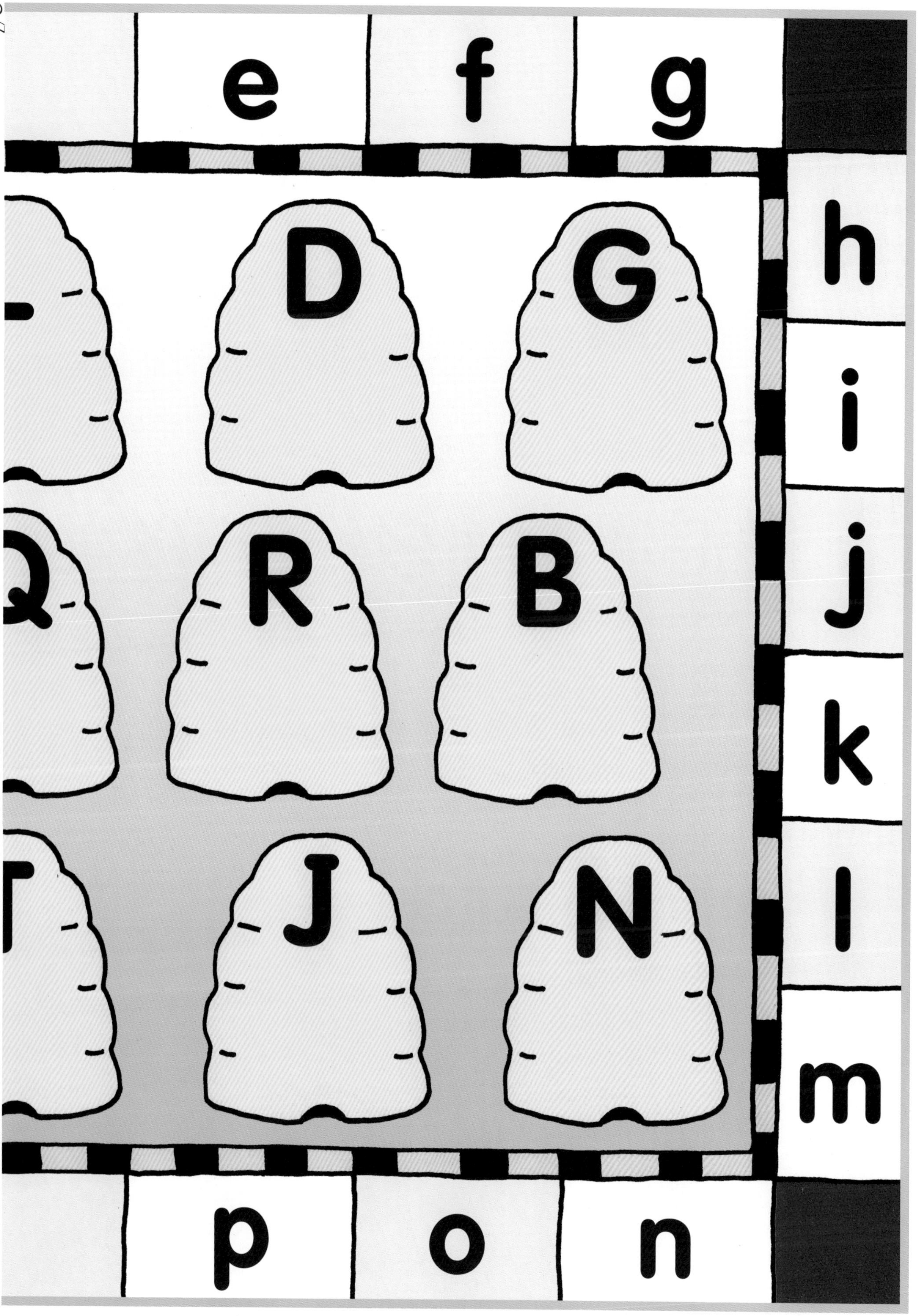

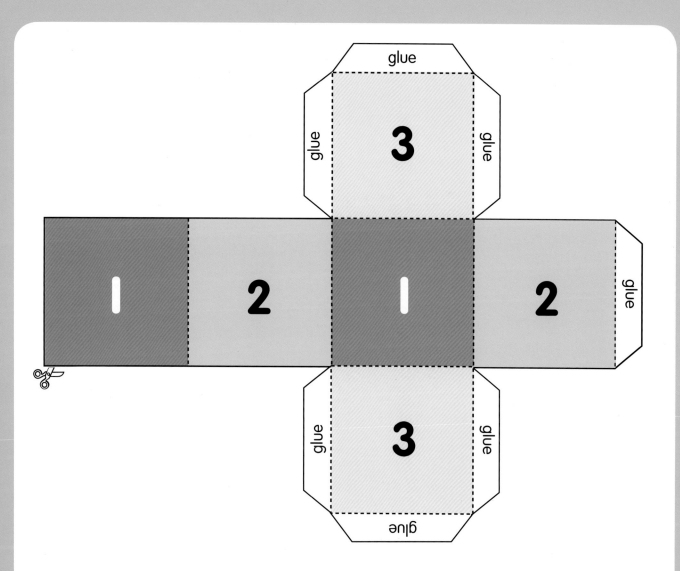

Fold the tabs on the game markers
so they stand up.

Fold here.

Fold here.

Fold here.

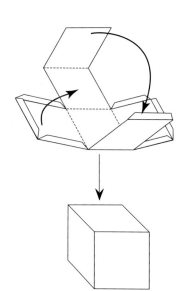

Assemble the cube by folding as shown. Glue closed.

Busy Alphabet Beavers

PLAYERS: 2-3

SKILL — This game provides practice in identifying uppercase and lowercase letters.

INTRODUCTION

Display an alphabet chart that shows each letter in uppercase and lowercase print. Point to a letter pair and ask children to identify the letter. Invite volunteers to identify the uppercase letter in the pair and then the lowercase. Afterward, point to letters at random and have children tell whether they are uppercase or lowercase.

ASSEMBLING THE GAME

1. Remove pages 51–59 from the book along the perforated lines. Cut out the file-folder label and pocket from page 51. Glue the label onto the file-folder tab. Tape the sides and bottom of the pocket to the front of the folder.

2. Cut out the directions and answer key on page 53. When the game is not in use, store these items in the pocket on the front of the folder.

3. Cut out the two sides of the game board on pages 55 and 57 and glue them to the inside of the folder.

4. Cut out and assemble the game spinner and game markers on page 59.

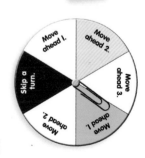

EXTENDING THE GAME

◎ Make a set of uppercase and lowercase letter cards to match the letters on the game board. Place the cards in a bag. Invite children to draw cards from the bag, name the letters, tell whether they are uppercase or lowercase, and then find the matching letters on the game board.

◎ Write each uppercase and lowercase letter in a letter pair on separate index cards. Hide the cards around the room. Then pair up children. Assign an uppercase letter to one child and the corresponding lowercase letter to his or her partner. Have children search the room to find their letters.

Busy Alphabet Beavers

GET READY TO PLAY

Each player places a game marker on Start.

TO PLAY

1 Spin the spinner. Follow the directions.

2 Name the letter you land on.
Is it a lowercase or uppercase letter?
Tell your answer.

3 Check the answer key. Is your answer correct?

- If so, leave your marker on the space.
- If not, move your marker back.

4 Keep taking turns. The first player to reach Finish wins the game.

PLAYING TIPS

- Players may land on and share the same space.
- Players must spin the exact number needed to move to Finish.

Busy Alphabet Beavers

ANSWER KEY

Lowercase letters:

a	b	d	e	f
g	h	j	k	m
n	q	r	t	

Uppercase letters:

A	B	D	E	F
G	H	J	K	M
N	Q	R	T	

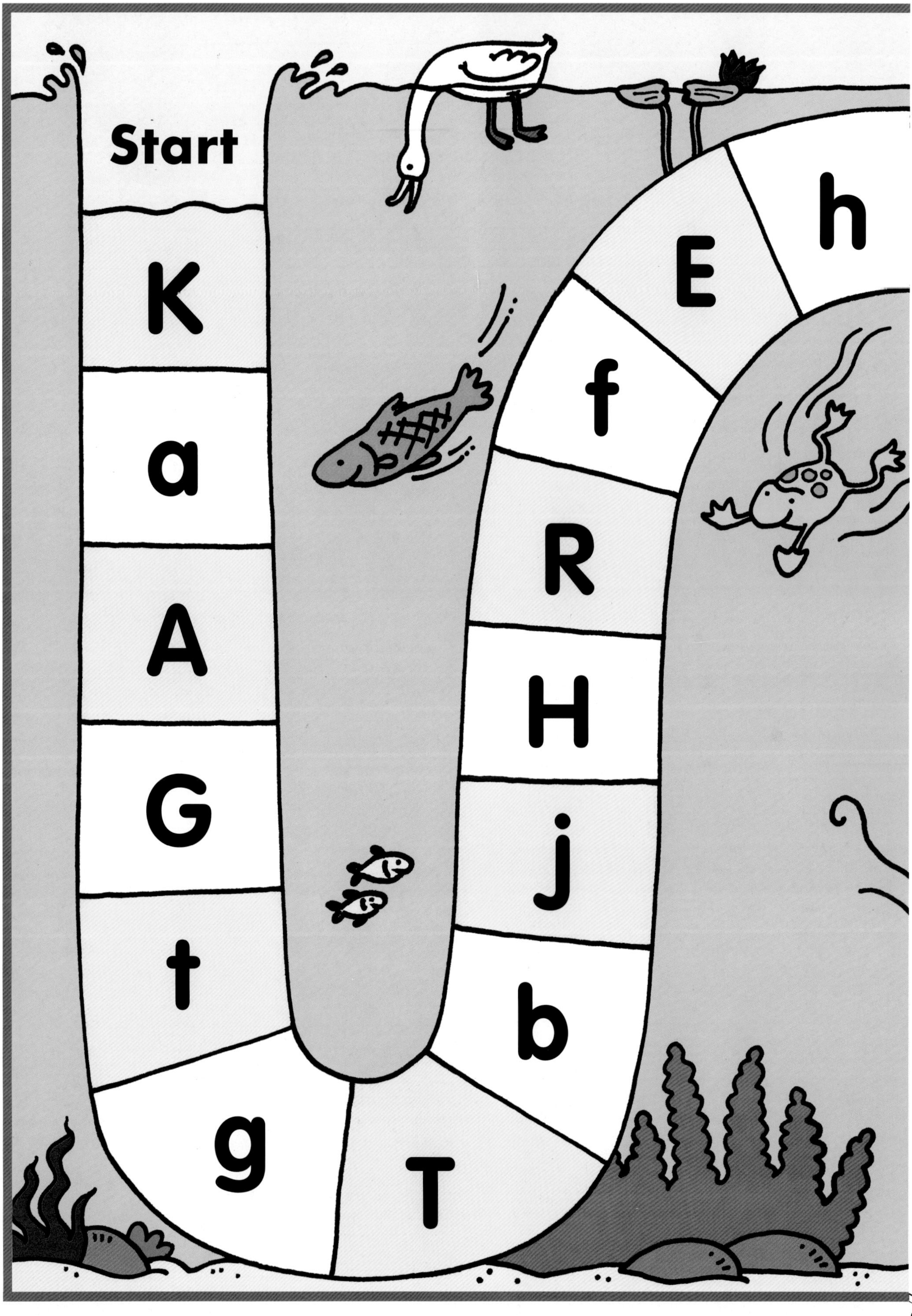
Start
K
a
A
G
t
g
T
b
j
H
R
f
E
h

Cut along this edge and attach to page 57.

Finish

Q
k
D
N
r
d
F
m

q
M
B
n
J
e

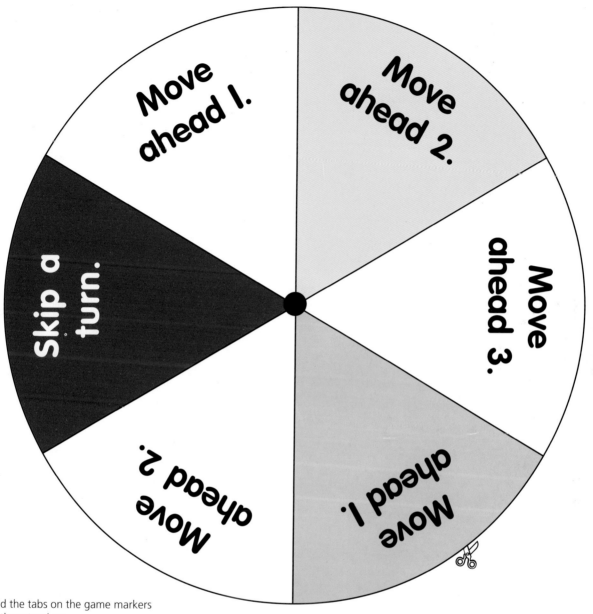

Move ahead 1.

Move ahead 2.

Move ahead 3.

Skip a turn.

Move ahead 2.

Move ahead 1.

Fold the tabs on the game markers so they stand up.

Fold here.

Fold here.

Fold here.

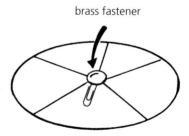

brass fastener

Assemble the spinner using a paper clip and brass fastener as shown. Make sure the paper clip spins easily.

Sky Writers

PLAYERS: 2

SKILL This game provides practice in writing uppercase and lowercase letters.

INTRODUCTION

Review the uppercase and lowercase letters of the alphabet with children. Then show them each game card. Ask them to name the picture and the letter it begins with. Finally, have them write that letter in uppercase and lowercase print on paper. You might have children refer to an alphabet chart as a writing guide.

ASSEMBLING THE GAME

1. Remove pages 63–73 from the book along the perforated lines. Cut out the file-folder label and pocket from page 63. Glue the label onto the file-folder tab. Tape the sides and bottom of the pocket to the front of the folder.

2. Cut out the directions, answer key, and game cards on pages 65, 67, and 73. When the game is not in use, store these items in the pocket on the front of the folder.

3. Cut out the two game boards on pages 69 and 71 and glue them to the inside of the folder.

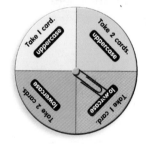

4. Cut out and assemble the game spinner on page 73.

Additional Materials Needed:
- two wipe-off pens
- paper towels

EXTENDING THE GAME

◎ Place the game cards in a paper bag. Invite children to draw a card from the bag, name the picture and its beginning letter, and then write that letter in uppercase and lowercase print.

◎ Have children write each letter in their first name in uppercase and lowercase print. Then have them find the game card that begins with each letter. Have them repeat the activity using the letters of their last names.

Sky Writers

GET READY TO PLAY

- Each player chooses a game board.
- Shuffle the cards. Place them facedown.

TO PLAY

1 Spin the spinner. Take that number of cards.

2 Name each picture. Tell what letter it begins with.
Then write that letter on a cloud.
Write the type of letter shown on the spinner: uppercase or lowercase.

3 After each turn, check the answer key. Did you write the correct letter for each card? If not, erase that letter.

4 Keep taking turns. The first player to fill in all of his or her clouds wins the game.

Sky Writers

ANSWER KEY

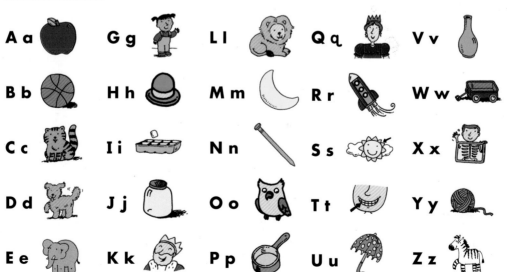

A a   G g   L l   Q q   V v

B b   H h   M m   R r   W w

C c   I i   N n   S s   X x

D d   J j   O o   T t   Y y

E e   K k   P p   U u   Z z

F f

More cards on page 73

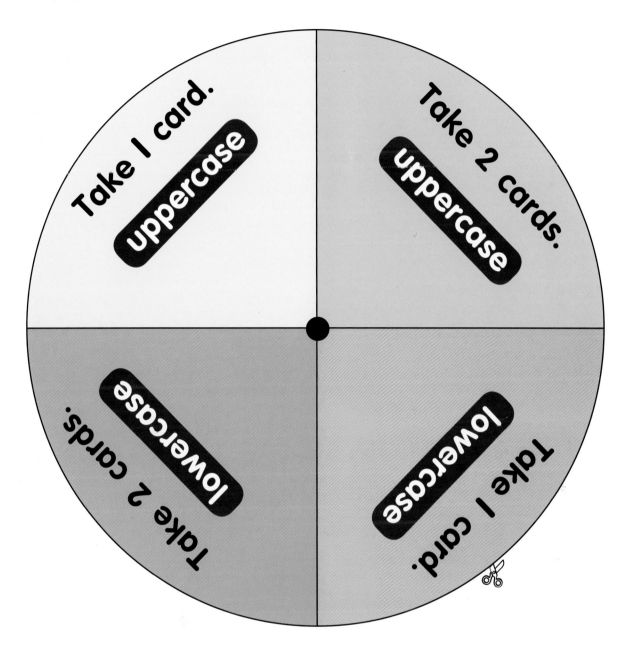

Take 1 card.
uppercase

Take 2 cards.
uppercase

Take 2 cards.
lowercase

Take 1 card.
lowercase

Game Cards

brass fastener

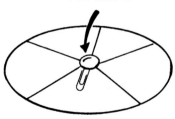

Assemble the spinner using a
paper clip and brass fastener as
shown. Make sure the paper clip
spins easily.

Line Up For Recess!

PLAYERS: 2

This game provides practice in sequencing words in alphabetical order.

INTRODUCTION

Point to one letter at a time, in sequence, on an alphabet chart. Have children identify each letter. Then show them each game card. Help children read the name on the card and identify the letter at the beginning of the name. Finally, have them put the cards in alphabetical order.

ASSEMBLING THE GAME

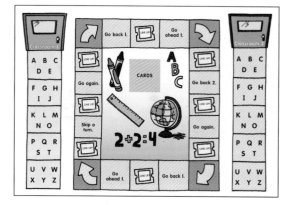

1. Remove pages 77–87 from the book along the perforated lines. Cut out the file-folder label and pocket from page 77. Glue the label onto the file-folder tab. Tape the sides and bottom of the pocket to the front of the folder.

2. Cut out the directions, answer key, and game cards on pages 79 and 81. When the game is not in use, store these items in the pocket on the front of the folder.

3. Cut out the two sides of the game board on pages 83 and 85 and glue them to the inside of the folder.

4. Cut out and assemble the game cube and game markers on page 87.

EXTENDING THE GAME

◎ Ask children to write their names on plain, white index cards. Then have small groups put their name cards in alphabetical order and check their work on an alphabet chart. Rearrange children into different groups and repeat the activity.

◎ Show small groups a sequence of 4–5 game cards arranged in alphabetical order, but with one card missing from the sequence. Ask children to search the remaining game cards to find the one that begins with the missing letter.

Line Up for Recess!

GET READY TO PLAY

- Each player chooses a game marker and a classroom on the game board. Place each marker on any arrow on the game board.

- Shuffle the cards. Stack them facedown on the game board.

TO PLAY

1. Roll the game cube. Move that number of spaces. Follow the directions on the space.

2. If the space has a ticket ⬚LINE UP!, take a card. Read the name. Does it begin with a letter on the top box in your classroom?
   - If so, place the card on the box.
   - If not, put the card on the bottom of the stack.

3. After each turn, check the answer key. Is your answer correct? If not, put the card on the bottom of the stack.

4. Keep taking turns. Cover the boxes for your classroom in order from top to bottom. The first player to cover all of his or her boxes wins the game.

PLAYING TIPS

- Players may land on and share the same space.

- Players may place only one card on each box in their classroom.

Line Up for Recess!

ANSWER KEY

A: Ann	**F:** Fred	**K:** Kate	**P:** Paul	**U:** Uma
B: Bob	**G:** Gina	**L:** Len	**Q:** Quincy	**V:** Vick
C: Cathy	**H:** Hans	**M:** Maria	**R:** Rose	**W:** Wilma
D: Dan	**I:** Ina	**N:** Nick	**S:** Sid	**X:** Xavier
E: Edna	**J:** Joe	**O:** Olive	**T:** Tammy	**Y:** Yvette
				Z: Zack

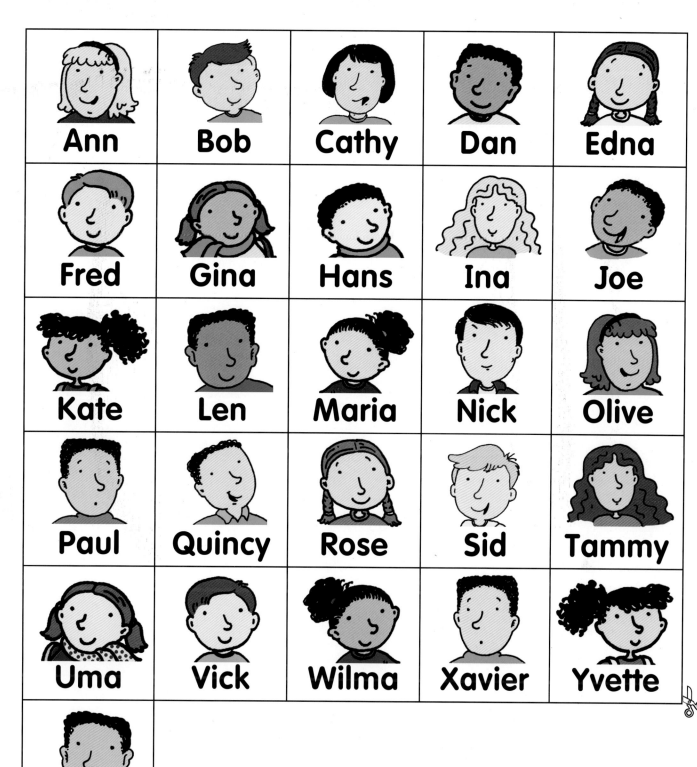

Ann	Bob	Cathy	Dan	Edna
Fred	Gina	Hans	Ina	Joe
Kate	Len	Maria	Nick	Olive
Paul	Quincy	Rose	Sid	Tammy
Uma	Vick	Wilma	Xavier	Yvette
Zack				

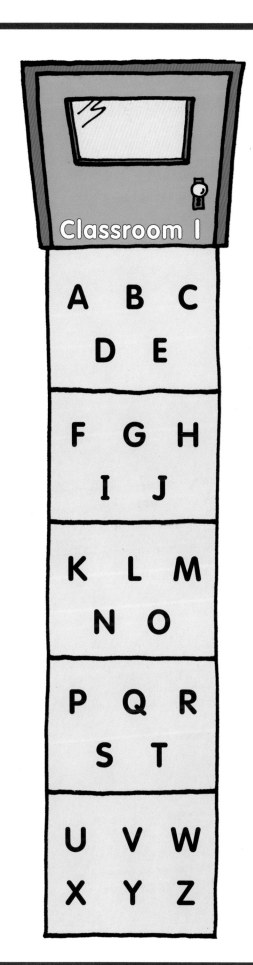

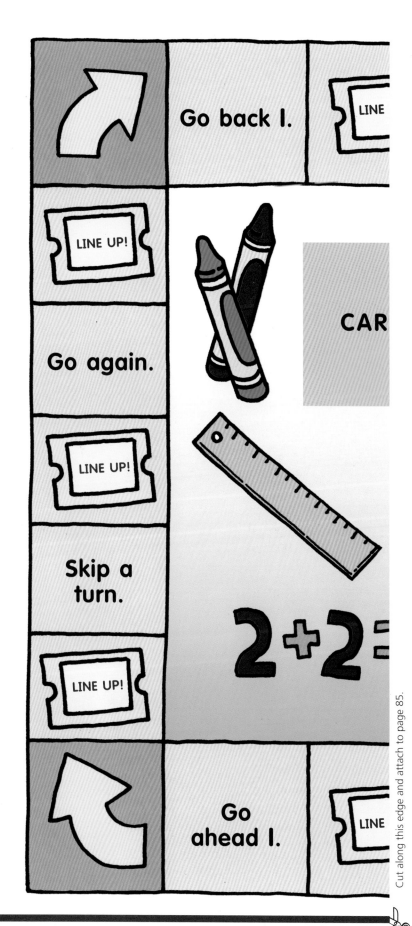

Classroom 1

A B C
D E

F G H
I J

K L M
N O

P Q R
S T

U V W
X Y Z

Go back 1.

LINE

LINE UP!

Go again.

LINE UP!

CAR

Skip a turn.

LINE UP!

2+2=

Go ahead 1.

LINE

Go ahead 1.

LINE UP!

Go back 2.

LINE UP!

Go again.

LINE UP!

DS

UP!

Go back 1.

UP!

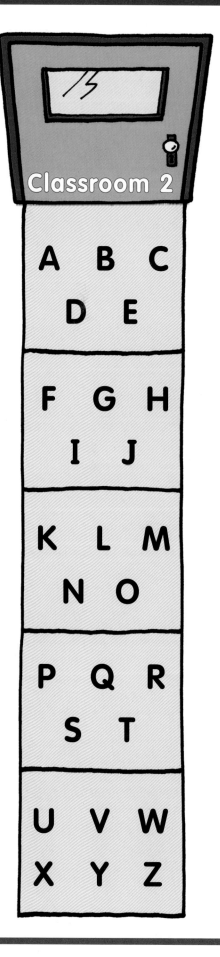

Classroom 2

A B C
D E

F G H
I J

K L M
N O

P Q R
S T

U V W
X Y Z

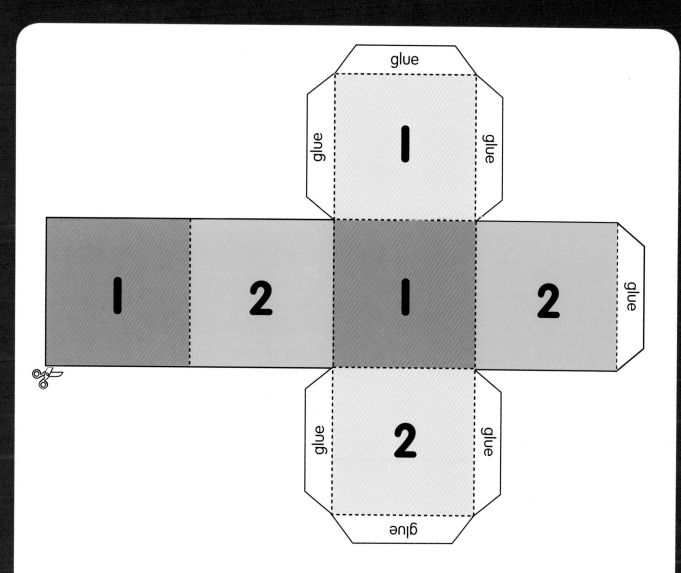

Fold the tabs on the game markers
so they stand up.

Fold here.

Fold here.

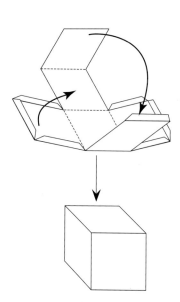

Assemble the cube by folding as shown. Glue closed.

Line Up for Recess! Game Cube and Game Markers

87

Consonants in the Castle

PLAYERS: 2

SKILL

This game provides practice with identifying initial consonants in words.

INTRODUCTION

Review initial consonant sounds with children. Show them each picture card from the game. Have them name the picture and identify the consonant sound at the beginning of the word. Ask children to brainstorm other words that begin with the same consonant sound.

ASSEMBLING THE GAME

1 Remove pages 91–103 from the book along the perforated lines. Cut out the file-folder label and pocket from page 91. Glue the label onto the file-folder tab. Tape the sides and bottom of the pocket to the front of the folder.

2 Cut out the directions, answer key, and game cards on pages 93, 95, and 97. When the game is not in use, store these items in the pocket on the front of the folder.

3 Cut out the two game boards on pages 99 and 101 and glue them to the inside of the folder.

4 Cut out and assemble the game cube on page 103.

EXTENDING THE GAME

◎ Choose 10 matching pairs of picture and jester cards. Invite children to use the cards to play Memory. To play, children flip two cards at a time to find the jester card that corresponds to the beginning sound of each picture card.

◎ Place the jester cards in a paper bag. Have children in a small group take turns drawing a card from the bag. Ask them to read the letter and then name a word that begins with that letter.

Consonants in the Castle

Consonants in the Castle

GET READY TO PLAY

- Each player chooses a game board and 10 picture cards.
  Put a picture card on each castle window.
- Shuffle the jester cards. Stack them facedown near the game boards.

TO PLAY

1 Roll the game cube. Take that number of jester cards.
If the cube lands on , take one card.
Then roll again and take that number of cards.

2 Name the letter on each card. Does a picture on your castle
begin with that letter?
- If so, take that picture off the window.
  Put the jester card on the window.
- If not, put the jester card on the bottom of the stack.

3 After each turn, check the answer key. Is each answer correct?
If not, put that picture back on the window.
Put the jester card on the bottom of the stack.

4 Keep taking turns. The first player to cover all of his or her
castle windows with jester cards wins the game.

Consonants in the Castle

ANSWER KEY

b: bed	**h:** hat	**n:** net	**t:** tub
c: can	**j:** jam	**p:** pig	**v:** van
d: dot	**k:** kiss	**q:** quack	**w:** wig
f: fan	**l:** log	**r:** rug	**y:** yell
g: gum	**m:** mop	**s:** sock	**z:** zip

Consonants in the Castle Game Cards, page 95

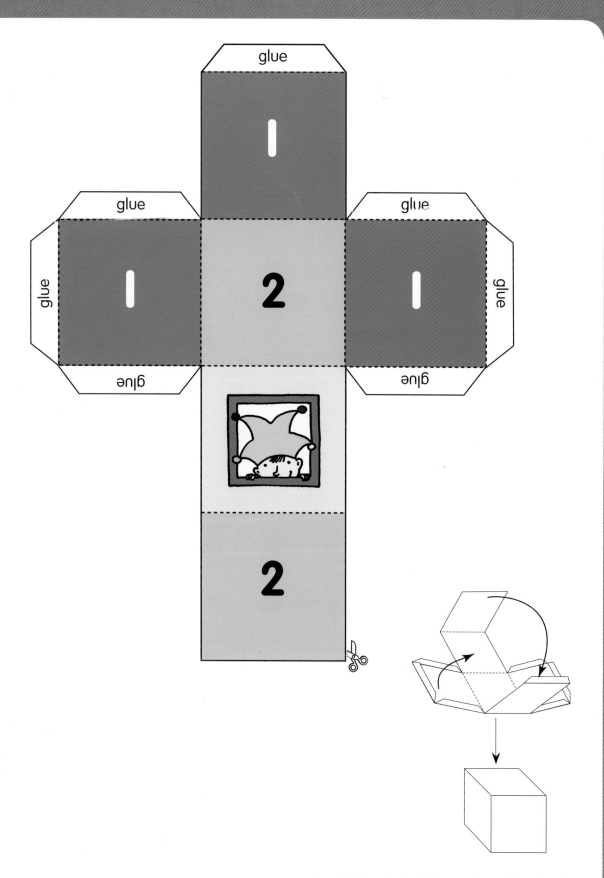

glue

glue

1

glue

glue

1

2

1

glue

glue

2

Assemble the cube by folding as shown. Glue closed.

Give a Pup a Bone

PLAYERS: 2-3

SKILL This game provides practice with identifying final consonants in words.

INTRODUCTION

Review final consonant sounds with children. Show them each picture card from the game. Have them name the picture and identify the consonant sound at the end of the word. Then challenge children to brainstorm other words that end with the same consonant sound.

ASSEMBLING THE GAME

1. Remove pages 107–117 from the book along the perforated lines. Cut out the file-folder label and pocket from page 107. Glue the label onto the file-folder tab. Tape the sides and bottom of the pocket to the front of the folder.

2. Cut out the directions, answer key, and game cards on pages 109 and 111. When the game is not in use, store these items in the pocket on the front of the folder.

3. Cut out the two sides of the game board on pages 113 and 115 and glue them to the inside of the folder.

4. Cut out and assemble the game cube and game markers on page 117.

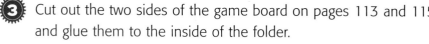

EXTENDING THE GAME

◎ Working with small groups, point to different consonants on your alphabet chart. Each time, ask children to name words that end in that consonant sound.

◎ Label each of several large sheets of white construction paper with a consonant. Invite children to search magazines and other sources to find pictures of items that end in the consonant sounds. Have them cut out the pictures and glue them to the corresponding pages.

Give a Pup a Bone

GET READY TO PLAY

- Each player places a game marker on any dog dish on the game board.
- Shuffle the cards. Stack them facedown on the game board.

TO PLAY

1 Roll the game cube. Move that number of spaces.
Follow the directions on the space.

2 If the space has a bone, take a card. Name the picture.
Then name the letter that makes the sound at the end of the word.

3 Check the answer key. Is your answer correct?
- If so, keep the card.
- If not, put the card on the bottom of the stack.

4 Keep taking turns. Play continues until all of the cards have been used.
The player with the most cards wins the game.

PLAYING TIPS

- Players may land on and share the same space.
- Players may move around the game board as many times as needed.

Give a Pup a Bone

ANSWER KEY

b: crab

d: bread, cloud

f: roof

g: frog, plug

k: brick, clock

l: shell, snail

m: drum, swim

n: clown, rain

p: ship

r: car, spider

s: glasses, grass

t: coat, hot

v: wave

x: mix, six

Go again.

CARDS

Go
ahead 1.

Go
ahead 1.

Skip a
turn.

Go
back 1.

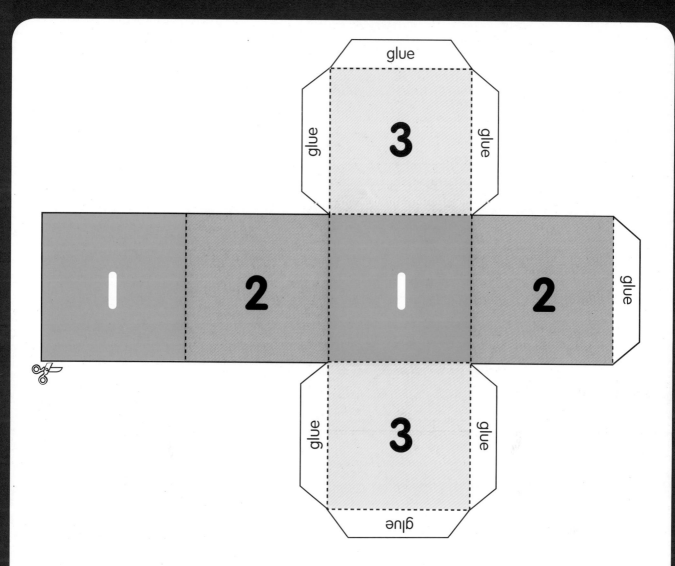

Fold the tabs on the game markers so they stand up.

Fold here.

Fold here.

Fold here.

Assemble the cube by folding as shown. Glue closed.

Short Vowel Picnic Ants

SKILL

This game provides practice with recognizing short vowels in words.

INTRODUCTION

Review short vowels with children. Show them each picture card from the game. Have them name the picture and identify the short vowel sound in the word. Afterward, ask them to group the pictures by vowel sounds. Finally, invite children to brainstorm other short vowel words and tell which group they go with.

ASSEMBLING THE GAME

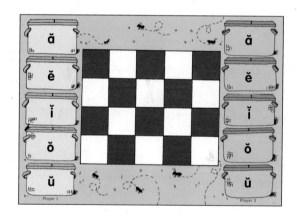

1. Remove pages 121–129 from the book along the perforated lines. Cut out the file-folder label and pocket from page 121. Glue the label onto the file-folder tab. Tape the sides and bottom of the pocket to the front of the folder.

2. Cut out the directions, answer key, and game cards on pages 123 and 125. When the game is not in use, store these items in the pocket on the front of the folder.

3. Cut out the two sides of the game board on pages 127 and 129 and glue them to the inside of the folder.

EXTENDING THE GAME

◎ Distribute the game cards to children. Have them assemble into groups according to the short vowel sounds represented by the pictures on their cards.

◎ Show children one game card at a time. Challenge them to name things they see around the room that have the same short vowel sound. For example, they might name items such as a backpack, desk, clip, box, and rug.

Short Vowel Picnic Ants

PLAYERS: 2

GET READY TO PLAY

- Each player chooses a set of picnic baskets on the game board.
- Shuffle the cards. Place each card facedown on a square.

TO PLAY

1 Pick two cards and flip them over. Name the pictures on the cards. Do they have the same short vowel sound?

- If so, place the match on the picnic basket for that vowel.
- If not, flip the cards back over.

2 After you make a match, check the answer key. Is your answer correct? If not, put the cards back.

3 Did you find a match for a basket that is already covered? If so, put the cards back. Then mix up the cards on the game board.

4 Keep taking turns. The first player to cover all of his or her picnic baskets wins the game.

PLAYING TIP

Players may flip only two cards on each turn.

Short Vowel Picnic Ants

ANSWER KEY

ă: back, clap, flag, tag

ĕ: bell, dress, hen, nest

ĭ: knit, swim, swing, witch

ŏ: block, drop, pot, stop,

ŭ: brush, bug, jump, truck

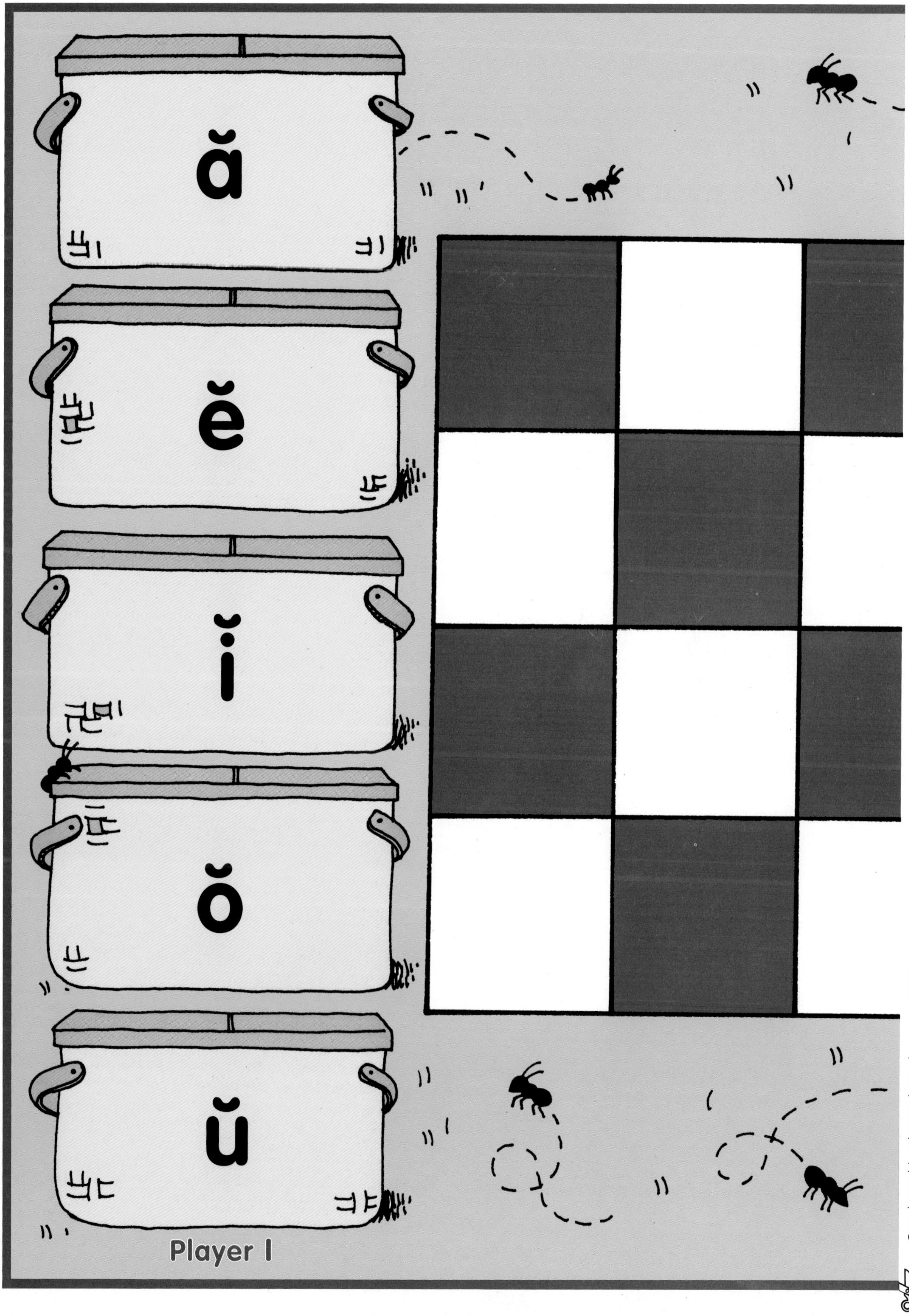

ă

ĕ

ĭ

ŏ

ŭ

Player I

Cut along this edge and attach to page 129.

Cut along this edge and attach to page 127.

ă
ĕ
ĭ
ŏ
ŭ
Player 2

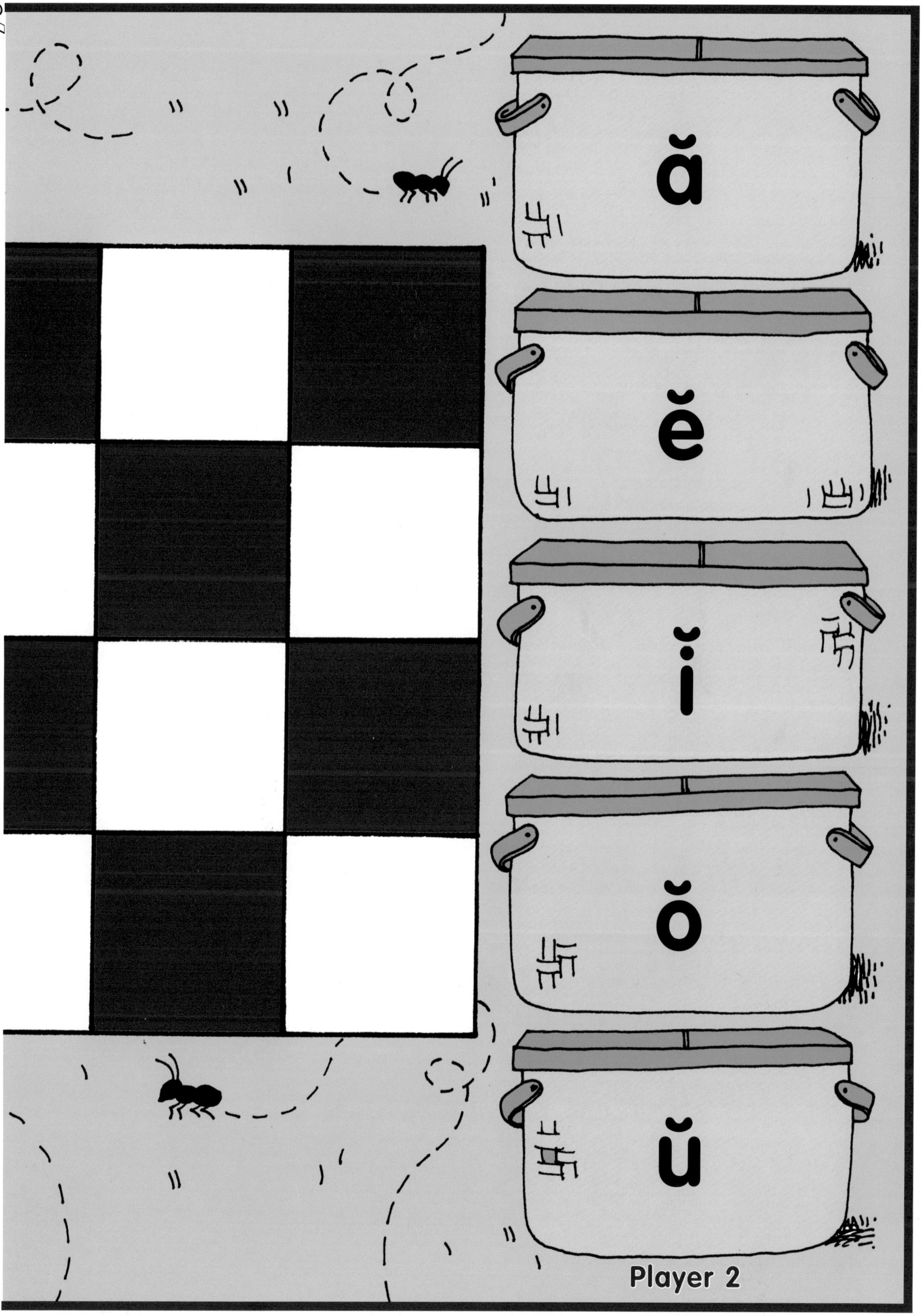

Short Vowel Picnic Ants Game Board (right side), page 129

Long Vowel Owl

PLAYERS: 2

This game provides practice in recognizing long vowels in words.

INTRODUCTION

Review long vowels with children. Show them each picture card from the game. Have them name the picture and identify the long vowel sound in the word. Afterward, ask them to group the pictures by vowel sounds. Finally, invite children to brainstorm other long vowel words and tell which group they go with.

Note: This game includes variant-vowel phonograms for the letter *u*.

ASSEMBLING THE GAME

1 Remove pages 133–143 from the book along the perforated lines. Cut out the file-folder label and pocket from page 133. Glue the label onto the file-folder tab. Tape the sides and bottom of the pocket to the front of the folder.

2 Cut out the directions, answer key, and game cards on pages 135 and 137. When the game is not in use, store these items in the pocket on the front of the folder.

3 Cut out the two game boards on pages 139 and 141 and glue them to the inside of the folder.

4 Cut out and assemble the game cube on page 143.

EXTENDING THE GAME

◎ Invite children to take turns showing one game card at a time to a partner. Have the partner name the picture and identify the long vowel sound in the word.

◎ To make new long-vowel picture cards to use with the game, have children cut out and glue magazine pictures to plain index cards. (They might also use clip-art pictures.) They can use counters to cover the boxes on their game boards.

Long Vowel Owl

GET READY TO PLAY

- Each player chooses a game board.
- Shuffle the game cards. Stack them facedown.

TO PLAY

1 Roll the game cube. Take that number of cards.
If the cube lands on 🦉, take one card.
Then roll again and take that number of cards.

2 Name the picture on each card. What long vowel sound do you hear?
Name it. Do you see that vowel on your barn?
- If so, put the card on the box.
- If not, put the card on the bottom of the stack.

3 After each turn, check the answer key. Is each answer correct?
If not, put that card on the bottom of the stack.

4 Keep taking turns. The first player to cover all of his or her
boxes wins the game.

PLAYING TIP

Players may place only one card on each box on their barn.

Long Vowel Owl

ANSWER KEY

$\bar{a}$: frame, skate, train, whale

$\bar{e}$: peach, sleep, tree, wheel

$\bar{i}$: dive, pie, slide, smile

$\bar{o}$: boat, nose, smoke, snow

$\bar{u}$: blue, boot, glue, spoon

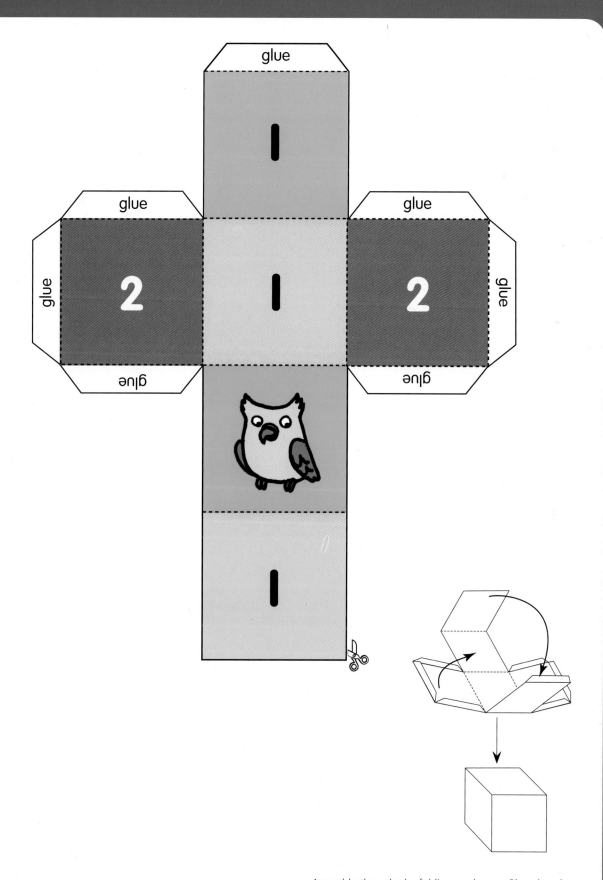

Assemble the cube by folding as shown. Glue closed.